Beneath the Deluge

Dear Catriona,
With much love
Catherine xx

CATHERINE M
BRENNAN

Cinnamon Press
Independent Innovative International

Published by Cinnamon Press
Meirion House, Glan yr afon, Tanygrisiau, Blaenau Ffestiniog,
Gwynedd LL41 3SU www.cinnamonpress.com

The right of Catherine M Brennan to be identified as author of this
work has been asserted by her in accordance with the Copyright,
Designs and Patent Act, 1988. © 2008 Catherine M Brennan
ISBN 978-1-905614-54-7
British Library Cataloguing in Publication Data. A CIP record for this
book can be obtained from the British Library.

Designed and typeset in Palatino by Cinnamon Press
Cover design by Mike Fortune-Wood from original artwork 'water
abstract 4' supplied by dreamstime.com

Acknowledgements

My particular thanks for close and generous readings to John Brennan,
Julia Copus, David Matthews, Richenda Power and Catherine Smith,
and to my editor, Jan Fortune-Wood. Also to all the 'Totters' and
Birkbeck University writers for inspiring times and sound advice. I am
deeply grateful to the Arvon Foundation for life changing weeks.

Some of the poems have previously been published, sometimes in
different versions, in *Iota, The New Writer, Other Poetry, Pulsar, Smoke,
Dream Catcher* and *Envoi.*

Biography:

Catherine M Brennan was born in Dublin and lives in London. She
works in education and is also a trade union case work officer for the
National Union of Teachers. She graduated with Honours in English
from the University of Sydney, and is currently studying for an MA in
Creative Writing at the University of East Anglia.

Contents

Westron wynde, when wilt thou blow,
The small raine down can raine.
Cryst, if my love were in my armes
And I in my bedde again!

Anon

*for my parents, Mary and Peter Brennan,
and for Jan Koene, for songs in dark times.*

Beneath the Deluge

Leaving the glen, with a white horse on a low boat

The Vikings have lost their spirit of adventure:
become three sad faced men, holding
the reins of a white horse as it stands in a low boat,
leaving the glen.

After forgotten years in the barn,
they are silenced, unable to clamour
in full blooded colour. A stain has colonised
one corner of the print. Their berserker yells
have failed to shift the weight and gilt of the frame.

Once, the burn of their eyes made children hide;
fear the rough sweep of wolf pelt cloaks
across the bedroom floor. They plundered
dreams, held the night hostage.

They fade now between monochrome borders
on the slow return from a naming, a wedding, a wake.
Or perhaps they are taking the horse to plough,
to market, to the knacker's yard.

From this distance, anything is possible.

Shorelines

As children, they'd hauled the bloated form
to shore in a net of seaweed, the thing's skin
bruising their finger tips like a blunted knife.

Prised apart, its belly revealed rows of eggs
nestled against the spine, gel sacs stiffening
from exposure to air.

Tonight he staunches the unpeeled gape
of his guts with a towel, the unsealed mass
held gently as new laid eggs.

The handiwork of one small, legal knife.
He tightens fists, fights tears that coalesce
with blood, brackish as seaweed.

View from Slieve Coillte

I look for the invisible lines
that divide counties – promised
six, or seven, or eight,
by the uncertain gate keeper,
who'd insisted I should climb
the hill before leaving, said
you won't regret it.

At sea level, surf thrashes
the headland, beats foam
into a turmoil of bubbles that scud
and rise as if alive, wild
white creatures cast
between salt and air.

The river flows stronger than the line
of roads,
until it diminishes, twists behind
the granite bulk of the Blackstairs Mountains:
formations from fire below the sea,
separations of water and rock.

I can't tell where one place begins
and another ends. The only boundaries
that matter on this rainy afternoon
are those of skin and air,
claims that keep you north of here.

Stranded

She splashes in shallows as the tide recedes,
reveals a new bauble washed by the foam,
stranded on the damp strip of shoreline.

Transparent membrane stretches thin, vivid
as bottled ink. A glass bubble just blown,
irresistible as it quivers at the water's edge.

If she leans down to lift it from the sand,
a cascade of fronds will descend, wrap
lacy edges around small fingers, set fire

to sudden welts that can not be kissed away.
I call her, hope the wind won't blow
the words to sea, before it's too late, hope

the sound of her name will be sufficient
to charm her from the man o' war,
the bluebottle, the thing she's yet to name.

Safely distant, we will watch the tender
sway and drift of those barbed tentacles,
as waves pull and lap at the dead weight.

Beneath the Deluge

November rain falls and falls:
we sleep to its beat,
wake to its patter and gurgle

in gutters and drain pipes,
a grey wash on the skylight.
We lie below glass below water;

trace shadows on the surface
of skin, release deeper currents.
Sunday morning dissolves.

Imagine, forty days and nights of it:
attic beams as ship's timbers,
these walls sturdy in heavy seas.

Adrift, we'd have no choice, would
rise and sink upon these waves,
follow the pull of new tides.

If we sent a dove flying, and she returned
with nothing at all, we could fall
toward the rhythms of this morning,

to time submerged; defined by rain.
We could dream again; drown again:
safe beneath the deluge.

Night drive, Kurnell Oil Refinery

We cruise toward the slop of black water
past sand dunes tough with marram grass,
air dirty with the dark smell of oil.

This landscape is made for painters
of mid century industrial shadows.
It's all cubes, cylinders, spaces lit

with strength and target like precision.
It's like a prison; the long perimeter
of barbs, electricity, chain metal.

Flames shoot and carve the night sky
with jagged rhythms. Seagulls coast
silently on currents high above floodlights.

Rotted plant life washes in on a slow tide;
we listen to the static crackle of the radio,
car windows wound up. The deep hum

of the refinery is in our bones,
its rhythm stronger than your heart beat.
It is time to go home; time to go.

Close up: Window with Crane Fly

Nothing but white sky,
damp press of mist. Stillness,
the space of your absence.

The day contracts. Clock ticks,
creak of floorboards. Colder air
and darker nights set in.

Outside: blank, familiar places.
On the window pane, a crane fly
flutters, one of the last of the season.

Each foot has its precise place
as she traces the arc of the circle
on the glass. She spins, pirouettes;

poised on the edge of falling
star shaped, snow flake slight,
as she falters then begins again.

Your plane casts shadows
on clouds, with you cocooned
above the blue. At this level,

the afternoon limps along:
the crane fly lurches, lifted
by light air into the next ellipsis.

Behind closed doors

This is the room
where she packed a suitcase
for a single journey.

Left her wedding veil
folded with yellow blossoms,
camphor and lavender.

Kept it in the bottom drawer,
preserved with the dried dust
of moth wings.

This is the room
where the click of the rosary
is the tick of the clock;

is precise seconds counted,
breaths measured like money
in short supply.

A wild wind swells
at the key hole, steers distant ships
to black rocks. The killing wind

moans: scours the room,
flicks curtain edges,
whips rain into corners.

This is the room
where the door is closed
when the telegram arrives.

This is the room
they filled with polished cabinets
displaying unused gifts.

This is the room they never filled.

Emigration, 1954

And he says he still misses the smell of grapes
growing warm in the afternoon sun,
the silk and spiked rustle of corn fields,
the sound of Rita's voice. Saturdays:
the *passeggiata* with views through
arches of stone; mountain roads
running toward Rome, *grappa* bitter
on his tongue, the morning
they were leaving home.

Now, he works to drown unknown valleys
with dams, breathes the ice of mornings
above the snow line; knows only that
these unfinished paths take him closer
to foreign horizons and skies bright
with constellations he can no longer name.

He recalls walking in olive groves,
collecting branches for blessing;
bringing armfuls to the church where
black clad women placed lilies for Easter,
the scent rising against thick myrrh.
And her *nonna's* whispered prayer,
to kneel with them again in the church
of *Sant' Chiara*, some future Sunday.

Van Gogh's Bedroom

for CB

Trop de détails effacent la rêverie-
                            Van Gogh

We save the house for last;
stubbled fields scrape ankles,
crows punctuate the sky.

The empty attic: warm air,
soft whirr of the projector
for the *son et lumière*.

Resonant, the absence
of his sleeping, breathing
spaces. Years later,

I find the room we'd missed:
plain bedstead, cold walls, ghost
of oils and cleaning fluids.

Serrations

Let the sweet acid rot
of citrus peel and apple core
lead to whoops and whistles

almost human calls
pitched behind the high walls
of the monkey house.

Walk eye level with the pattern of bars
set in a curve of green concrete.

The world is serrated:
black and white zebras,
black and white signs.

An open space:
familiar mulch. Straw.
Farm smells. You know these things.
This must be safe.

Step closer, climb.
The slip of fists leaves sweat on metal.

Stretch and press on tiptoe,
wedge your feet between the bars,
scuff new shoes.

Securely lodged, you will not fall.
Can not move.
Peer to the far blackness:
nothing.

Nothing wakes,
senses you. Stirs and shifts,
fluffs its sharpness out.

Dark quills on dark fur,
a jaw runs the hungry length of its body.

Nothing grows:
hisses, clicks, taps,
claws on the move...

twitching toward you
blinking from the shadows,
the first of the porcupines emerges:

sniffs, pauses,
harmless in sunlight.

Valentine's night

St Stephen's grave yard; we've left
the party and it's raining: a drizzle drips
through the leaves of a wide arching tree.
Roots slowly disturb surrounding head stones;
reclaim earth. Below us, someone
from eighteen fifty something is original dust.

Your jacket is between me and damp earth,
and you're above, holding your weight
carefully as unwritten music; you hold
yourself between me and a night sky
full of rain. We both breathe: soft sounds
in a city church yard; soft sounds
as we lie on consecrated ground.

A hard faith

The shrines dominated the city, we think. Whole
streets of temples competed for the adoration

of the devout. At certain times of year pilgrims
slept outside, waited to be the first to pay homage.

We imagine it must have been auspicious,
for them to shiver through mid winter's nights.

Appointed guardians performed seasonal rituals,
garlanded altars with durable, unfading flowers.

Sometimes worshippers congregated in daylight
to watch the neophytes bless the sacred items.

Or reliquaries were decorated after dark, secretly,
seen only by the sleepless eyes of unbelievers.

Were these nocturnal events intended to punish
the lapsed, or to entice them back to the fold?

All we can state with certainty, is that these
were their gods. Observe their glossed perfection,

eternally smooth skin, smiles painted indifferent
to hope and suffering. They lack human proportions:

are immaculate mannequins. They must be gods.

First night apart

His last night in the country
and he's breaking the law
like a joyless teenager.
The collar is turned on his new coat,
cap pulled against raw mountain rain.
Her words tug: *can't you let this go.*

He clenches wire cutters,
makes the first gentle snick
near the blackness of hazels;
his ungloved fingers
feel the answering spring
of wire released, a click
softer than the night jar.
He eases the strands apart,
loops the edges back with care,
like a man who has all night.

The softness of damp breath
is the sleeping mass of sheep.
He calls; hushes; they follow.
For hours he moves that sea of fleeces,
all eyes alike on a moonless night:
liquid, depthless, dumb.

The embers are dull.
She mends a small rip in his coat;
he smokes in silence. Between them,
the dog: wrapped in a blanket,
coat brushed. He's done his best
to straighten the spasm of limbs,
to wipe the muzzle clear
of the sour spew of poison.

He says, *the mad bastard will think again*
before he blames dogs for the work of foxes.

Stargazers, Hong Kong

for CB

The season's first typhoon has yet to break:
fan blades swish all night in thick air,
stir the humidity.

Overblown lilies fill the small flat
with their peppery scent, scatter a burst
of orange stains as we brush past.

You bought them in the last hour at the market,
near the song birds in bamboo cages;
cradled them through the crush of the metro,

dust of the street. A salt breeze across
the Star Ferry deck is too brief:
walking uphill we wilt, are sapped.

Rains sweep through my dreams, a cascade
rushes the narrow length of Stanley Street,
washes away the endless heat.

Waking, I find it is only the sound
of the filter bubbling in the fish tank:
nothing has changed.

The gold fish swim undisturbed,
peer through the sway of green fronds
toward the lilies, magnified.

I'm reminded of Matisse, the Sunday
we'd queued for hours in unexpected Parisian
heat. And the woman in mauve

who'd waited so quietly, only to face
that brilliant explosion of poppies
before fainting. The sweetness

of these real flowers is heady too;
their scent carries below, to where
old men wait in evening doorways.

Samhain

i.m Timothy 'Bud' Howell, 1960-1981

your ghost shadows these streets

bonfire flames
snap
night air
defy the darkness

there is time to blaze

we lean closer
seduced by danger &
promises

skin
hunger consumes

at nineteen
you pour kerosene
on flames
fearless

later, we watch ash
flaking
on an east wind

into the cold of ordinary mornings

the spaces between fire light
& shadows
shifting

such traces linger in dreams

when you & I
flicker

before we are embers

Beyond the Pale

Lawless against a lowered sky,
jackdaws curve above a disused church,
darken the air with their *tchaks*
between spits of rain.

We take the contours of bloodlines,
follow old paths, leave all we ought
to know. Home lights glimmer,
a bright ring on the distant bay.

Wind rises, teases the surface
of the lough, black with the freeze
of mountain water, brown
with the blood stain of peat.

Words fail; heat beats
compel us further and higher
beyond the pale,
where we may be ourselves, untied.

Suspended transmission

Lost texts condense to cloud
taut with bruised echoes
thunder in August

messages rise to high cirrus
fail to cross the width
of these rivers, this sea:

I miss you, miss you still
not a word arrives.

Hail shots burst from nimbus
pelt apart stretched hours
chill when the sky has cleared

plane fumes crystallise as white
contrails, clear cut promises
etched against the blue

until the lines fade and curl
a scribbled drift of water
language we can't decipher.

Hollows

They slide between their skins
and sleep; blackness pulses
between eye and eye lid.

A southerly breeze slips,
twists the mosquito net,
dries salt on damp fingers.

Bodies starfish the bed,
hold the red memory,
the surprise of kisses

in the softest of places,
a half remembered tongue:
the certainty of caresses.

They lie in echoes, whisper
prayers to the gods of darkness
to hold the moment

as soundly as an old tree holds earth
in the hollows if its base.

Constancy

i.m. Edward Brennan, 1931-2003

We heard it before we knew what it was,
rhythm strong as a piston engine,
echoing along the river. Curving low
around a bend of the Arun: the swan,
wings and heart hammering, propelled
by the strength of the sound.

*

The sterile quiet of the fourth floor wing:
his heart beat unfailing, out of time
with those closed eyes and still hands.
Tubes carry breath, amplify
with a strength he does not possess.

Sometimes, he seems to blink,
as if recalled to our time, but
it's no more than a trick of the light.
There are only sounds between us.
His heat beats on, constant
as if he had need of it yet.

*

We live at the mercy of flight times
when we are called across the water.
Landing, we walk against the wind
on the tarmac, queue in silence.
Distance reduces like closing light
above swans on an evening river.

The Original Marble Dance Theatre

You've seen what's left of the curtains
in your museum, of course:
polished folds of carrara, looped
with all the grandeur of velvet,
and none of the decay.

The seats are pure porphyry,
transported from the next province
with great difficulty, we imagine, but
you'll agree it gives the effect of warmth.

The pillars are replicas, I'm afraid,
no more than painted wood. Best
not to touch, it spoils the illusion.

Listen: sometimes, they say you can hear
the rasp of pumice against tender feet,
the scrape of sandpaper, preparing the dancers.

Hamsa

The hamsa *hand is an Arabic amulet which gives protection from the evil eye.*
In Hebrew, it is hamesh

Sometimes we see it coming, yet falter
in the white glare, transfixed and flightless.
To hold our hearts' weight alone from harm
demands such balance, when life is pared

clean to the bone; with air between us,
a hand span apart. Rain blurs headlights,
black as taxis taking the night-sweats
of strangers to their separate mornings.

Across fractured states, the current
creates a vivid impulse to connect:
place palm to palm; trace fingertips.
Let the transient arc of the pulse leap,

limitless. No safe place, but kisses lie
like a fugitive gift: a charm of light.

Crossing Niagara Falls

At the end I stand before you, free.
Each step is taken once:
to falter is to fail.

The balance is in the mind,
feet have nothing to do with it.
I am across before I have begun.

Do I fear falling? ...

It would be a flight, wingless,
through cold air and into colder water
from one element to the next.

Weather Talk

for JB

River and road run parallel, where
we pass the snake institute, practising
counting to ten: *neung, song, sam...*

Mornings are rich with the scents
of crushed coriander, hot peanut oil,
incense rising against traffic fumes.

Afternoon storms sweep in, and we
shelter where small lamps reflect gold
from a Buddha reclining in fragrant air.

Seen between the slants of rain,
the river is a sea of water hyacinth
slapping the sides of stilted houses.

We smoke the last damp *Krong Thip*,
try our text book weather talk; your smile
always more accurate than your tone.

Street stalls re-appear, jewelled
with the neon of pink and lime sweets.
Prayer bells half chime as raindrops

fall from their edges. You begin to talk
to strangers, share delight when words
open worlds as easily as temple doors.

Breaking the Surface

a silver flicker
pierces the moment of waking

the hook slides invisible
into flesh, cleaves

inner and outer lip
catches the tenderness

of a cheek, raises
a welt below one eye

the dry slap of air
is a blow to the head

steel slices the underbelly
of sleep. Return:

five breaths more,
and the space of water

Centurion's legacy

Bones, sword, breast plate,
sandals. All that's left
laid bare: his strengths and scars.
Little of his loves, all of his wars.

No warmth now from hands
that signalled orders to legions
shivering in a foreign valley
as he marched steady, measured
along the frozen line.

When distant orders came to leave
the wall, his pension was secure
after twenty six years;
something saved in barbarous times.
Or were these cold adventures
for some northern love?

He has become these labelled lengths
of leather, iron and bone: the hazel eyes
and olive skin of the farmer
who directed us further, toward
this crumbling stretch of Hadrian's wall.

Alice, tumbling

After a painting by Charles Blackman

Drowning in a sea of midnight daisies,
this girl's in eternal spin,
perpetually falling.

Eyes half closed
she catches the blurred bar
of light above, her last view
of real time seen
through the glow of white flowers
that should not be open.

Threnody: afternoon tea

i.m. Catherine Clare Sexton 1911-2006

She likes the way light filters
the fine china of the cup
before I pour smoky tea,
and we try cakes sweet
with slices of peach.

Worth coming from London for,
she says: I agree.

She talks of sunrise, seen
beside the pilot of a 747
as it flew over Singapore;
the size of the curve of the earth.

Of elections, ways to cast
your vote, and what her dreams
might mean, these nights.

Along disinfected corridors, strangers
shuffle, a radio plays tunes
from the wrong era,
constant counterpoint to silence.

We will hold to the lightness of china,
to the hard length of this afternoon.

The Dynamics of Collision

It's much less than perfect,
but way better than random.

Find all the positions for binding
specific, short motifs,
those subtleties of affinity.

Charms can be found
in nearly every aspect of Science:

dozens of fist sized ghosts
sunshine monks
dragons of twine and ribbon.

The ultimate size
of a seismic rupture
is largely controlled
by the underlying fault.

Living cells need regulatory processes
of great sensitivity
have complex signalling pathways
must maintain fidelity.

The solution cannot be explained
in terms of tightly bound,
enduring molecular complexes.

Allow time
to become re-orientated,
re-positioned.

Fit together more tightly,
cover new ground.

Leftovers

Dozens of fist sized ghosts blow in on a wind
deafening as the mistral,
slam then slub against the glass,
squash their transparency into view.

Submerged in the press of creatures
pale and tough as jellyfish, we try
to identify features: your eyes, my mouth,
some unsettled fusion of both of us
in a smaller one, sunk grey
at the base of the kitchen window pane.

What gods did we fail to feed,
that we are at the mercy of this surge of ghosts?
Small mouths in constant movement,
the spite of their mews
scrapes a hunger we cannot ease.

Sunshine monks

Once you have placed your suitcase by the door
and you lie sleeping, I will take scissors
to every newspaper in the house:
cut out sunshine monks,
hundreds of them.

Their squat shapes will be emblazoned
with rugby results, the Dow Jones index, warnings
of freezing fog and strikes in distant airports…
and I will sing softly to them,
invoke their powers of warmth and light,
threaten decapitation should they fail.

As you dream,
I will tiptoe onto a chair,
stretch to the top of the window pane
begin to cover and seal the draft
with a barrier of monks.
If you hear the sash rattle,
you will think it is the wind, as always,
and sleep on.

Once the blankness of the window
holds their forms, ink smudged
by the damp of seeping frost,
I will climb over you
and begin below the coving,
papering a frieze around the room,
a border of charms.

February darkness will end,
rivers will swell with the thaw of snow.
In the surprise of morning, pilots
will wake from dreams of Icarus,
smell the singed ghosts of feathers and wax
beneath the fuselage.

They will opt to stay grounded,
flights cancelled for the first time in history
due to an excess of sunshine.

The pond requires a victim

i

One hand is a vice, clamps
the squiggle slit closed

spawn solidifies, chokes
bubbles below

the day throbs astringent
green as poison

dry eyed, he releases the grip
and squeeze on damp skin

lets silence sink to mud.

ii

Silence. Mud oozes
between toes, silts black deposits
in the folds of skin, clings.

Broken glass glints in the darkness,
disturbs root beds. Willow branches
trap the shreds of blue plastic bags.

The day stagnates.

iii

White limbs scissor dark water
slice foam and scum
cut a wake of acid green.

Osiers are fingers, caress
and anchor submerged twists-
metal, angled to kiss

bite bare skin within seconds.

iv

This is the place: I know the abandoned
thing strewn in the dried thickness
of last Summer, spokes rusting now.

Darkness stabs undergrowth.

I hesitate to claim that afternoon,
acknowledge this barbed time.
Mine: never mine.

Chittaway Point

For my parents

River smells rise
dank and promising
late warm evening:

I'm back in the tall grass
that brushed knees,
surrounded the fibro house

where evening sounds
echoed across the stillness

over shelved depths
that rippled around the submerged tree
where every swim was careful
every dive reckless

that final night,
walking on a road so dust filled and dry
that the giant lizard blocking our path
was an ochre shadow
unblinking and unreal

something from another time
remembered like a dream.

Cloudless vision

She finds the world: a pebble slips underfoot,
dust rises, spiced with the warmth of horses.

In her mind, the remembered landscape looms:
a vastness of steppes, boulders, plains, craters
white lined from the salt of inland seas
that did not last.

Wheat masses, sways in ghostly fields.
Armies march as a distant rumble in the wind,
the rasp of goat bells the nearest sound.

Smoke tickles from the brazier, black ice
crackles, settles on the high ground.
Her hands are guided around the first bowl
of thick tea. Later, she will wash and tease wool,
let lanolin grease the crevices of her skin.

Passing, her grandson waits:
she plucks a loose thread from his coat,
winds it around her finger, wears it ring like;
a fine line of scarlet she feels,
unseeing.

February days

I crush particles of ice beneath bare feet
turn these stones to feel the earth
tease and turn and pluck
this barren soil to find
even one green shoot
to coax and cavil
into life

I remember her
stooping
framed

in the tunnel's embrace
pomegranate clutched
uneaten and ripe

these mornings I take dust
from the hearth
to scatter on resistant ground

sweep the grate so hard
a flat blister forms
between thumb and forefinger

when I peel back the skin
there is no sting
at first

air on nerve
and then
a burst of pain

I am forced into feeling

while she

is still breathing
in that fetid world below.

Speechless

He crumbles earth,
dry clods fall.

Gives a blank face,
blank sounds

to strangers, to the lens
of the camera.

He stumbles in mud,
spills well water.

In his father's house:
silence.
No one speaks his name.

Crossing Bridges

for my father

That April day is kept in black and white:
walking home, kit bag and rifle by his side,
a street photographer called; he stopped mid-stride;
face caught in shadow, turning toward the light.

In a lane beyond the bridge and years before,
his father watched the dust from rubble rise,
saw black smoke choke spring time skies,
shouldered the weight of an unused gun, and swore

his sons would know these streets by other names.
And I, watching the brown river flow, wait
as you adjust the meter to control the light,
define the street within the camera's frame,
comment on the bridge's span and height
as if these measurements were black and white.

Facing the drought

After her doctor's visits he stoops, slower
in the arid afternoons of drawn out summer.

He leans across the neatness of his hedge,
I don't know what I'll do, when she's gone.

Roses struggle, bright in the small formality
of the front garden. He carries the watering can

through the house, patient while earth cracks,
fails to absorb anything but the hardest of rains.

He can only wait, as root systems are revealed,
stripped by fault lines that deepen each day.

He cannot escape the drowning

The cold skirl of a green sea
closes above, although he walks
these final days far from salt inlets
and estuaries alive with the black calls
of gulls and winter geese.

He breathes the vivid scent
of late wild sorrel, sees rowan
berries cluster and swell,
bright as fire against a clear sky.

None of it is ever enough
to banish the imagined pitch
and roll of timbers hewn to hold
their crew from harm, crafted
not to yield their cargo to the waves.

He kneels on the cool solidity
of stone floors in the chancel,
feels a ghost wind chill his neck.
His promise echoes along the nave:

to keep the shore line beacon lit,
warning for sailors unable
and unwilling to swim
to save themselves
from the claim of water.

He lights candles
against the outer darkness
keeps these small flames burning.

Rainbow Street, Amman

for RAH

Suspended between Rainbow Street
and Mango Street, the city:
clustered houses, hills and dry heat.

A glimpse of Roman citadel
reflects white where roads meet
like dry rivers in the distance.

Even as dust thickens the air
and grit rises to sting, you walk
through Sunday afternoon

as if you were not stepping
on the fallen stones of fallen empire.

The boatman to his lover, October 1834

When I saw that great bruise of blue
at the centre,
saw the whole thing engulfed: Lords, Commons
all ablaze,
reflected firelight dancing in your eyes
as you stood by the water's edge–

I knew, for the first time in years
I'd be warm tonight.

Not the familiar sweat of our bed,
but a bone drying blaze to remember.

Some September mornings
river breath snakes into my lungs,
shapes my dreams
where eels twist in tidal hollows
and you lie restless, damp beside me.

These flames, these sparks
that rise and singe the air

your smile as glass explodes
between the falling stones–

I would have paid for this, for this alone.

Dawn swim

You always wait for me to dive first.
I never ask why; just plunge…

We code the coldness by numbers:
closest to ten is when icy depths

are breath taking: You have to move
or go under in this blue space.

To shiver free of that freeze, I want
to race you, push hard and steady

against the shock of water, knowing
you will win, each limitless morning.

Transformation

I began with small details:
hairs on the chin.

Coarser, thicker, more wiry.
The grey worked well,
had a lupine quality to start with.

People were too polite to comment, of course.

Nails to claws next:
surprisingly easy, actually.

I practised using my hands less and less
for human purposes. Stopped knitting –
a relief, after years of gloves, scarves, socks,
Christmas gifts they all winced at...

–thought my eyes
weren't sharp enough to see their faces.

I rest my paws on the coverlet,
admire my pelt. Wait for the next full moon.

Agrotis infusa: nocturnal cycles

above, the moon changes
crescent to full to darkness
below, moths pupate
black soil plains give birth
in winter:

instars emerge,
cutworms raze seedlings
feed on wheat, barley, lucerne,
land dusted with arsenic

Summer storms build
barometric pressure drops
each imago must migrate
seek crevasses
Alpine caves

fly on nectar from flowering gums

drawn off course by lights
cities as other suns
magnetic

too early to aestivate
they shed scales on public
buildings
a grime of dust
sticks
smells crushed, bitter

you turn away
shadows brush over
as you sleep

sometimes your breath is so slow
it's a strain to be sure
you are still there

distant gear changes grind
a tin can clatters in the gutter
a brief rattle like rain

humidity drags
4a.m.: I sit on the steps,

wish for a cool change

for light to sharpen
the blur of lifeless grapevine
to an arabesque

petrol and city dust
crushed to night smells

when I return
you lie cocooned

a twist of sheets

all sweat and moonlight

Transit of Venus

for JD

Today, blindingly, Venus crosses the Sun.
So many revolutions on, the earth has spun;
we've pinned eclipses through paper,
formed shadow puppets from changing skies.

Late days of Autumn saw us wait
for one night when the distant line
of the Pacific's swell would merge
invisible into sky, when a blaze
of comet tail might be revealed.

One dawn, we watched the turn of desert skies
from pale to burning blue, saw the same day fade
to shadows and to twilight. And once,
above Jakarta's haze and hum, we drank
to the wildness of lightning, to storm filled hours
stopped by equatorial night.

On the hills of a dry state, or in a city by the river;
claiming new lands leaves a rough constancy.
The usual questions remain, with sometime
dreams of comets in southern skies,
eclipses in northern ones,
what's left between.

Amber

This is how it begins:

a single drop
seductive as wild honey
setting on the bark of an oak.
Resinous. It draws you in.

It holds: first a wing,
fluttering, failing; then limbs,
drenched in amber.

Forests submerge:
northern seas wash; preserve.
Struggle? No sign of it,
where filaments lie defined in gold,
the flight of lace wings forgotten.

Only air will reveal the surface,
crack the glaze, conceal
the heart of it in time.

The Astronaut's Cat

Astronauts lose bone density when exposed to zero gravity.
Exposure to certain frequencies of hertz can help stimulate bone density.
Cats purr within this frequency range.

He prowls the hum of blank corridors;
sniffs for the musty promise of mice.
Sleek plastic smells pervade: sealed units
refuse to yield. Contained cables
can not be wrestled into fresh tangles,
resist his games. Only interior doors
slide open. Exploration is confined.

Denied release, he accepts a pat,
settles on a lap, lulled toward sleep.
He allows the music of his purrs to heal
and strengthen his human's bones, so they
may both walk again in a weighted world.

He dreams: places where whole fields
full of mice lie waiting beneath open skies.

Crescendo: love, not love

For me, it began on a humid Tuesday morning when the milk curdled, and the baby, recovering from croup, began to cough again, a hard crackle splitting her chest like the hiss of a radio tuned to the edge of the station. And when I went to turn the radio off, the high pitch in the kitchen that was grating my teeth and scraping my spine continued seconds after the power was gone... Out of the corner of my eye, a glimpse of cheap velvet and brash satin, and the first of the sopranos scuttled out of sight behind the rosemary bush. I could not have known then that this was just the beginning of those terrible times, and far more than personal hallucinations after a night of too much cheap red wine.

By Friday, they were increasing in boldness, leaving droppings on the lawn: uncurling periwigs, gloves, love letters. On the car door handle, a smear of pancake make up. Worst of all, their infectious tunes, piercing our brains, pushing new rhythms into our blood streams, making simple conversations impossible. Marriages began to crack under the strain of dominant fathers in law, jealous husbands and errant wives. Butchers leered, bakers fondled rising yeast in an excess of fumbling. The barber's shop was hideous: a queue of all our young men lost to the lure of the Don Juan number one haircut.

And the creatures fed on our misery and discomfort, began to appear in daylight, growing fat and round voiced. Bass tones swelled in supermarket aisles, drowned out the Tannoy on thinning railway platforms. They thronged, mumbled and rumbled their words, *Amore, non amare...* Their hunger consumed our silences.

The worst of it was when their parasites began to appear, breeding in the driveway, blocking the gutters. Resting cellos and violins spiked their bows into the ankles of pedestrians, tripping the short sighted and infirm, cutting with cacophonous injury. Falls were usually fatal, beginning with a ringing in the ears, a swelling of the throat, uncontrollable panting and a fierce thirst for Spanish wine...